I
THANK
GOD

Mabel A. Chang

Trilogy Christian Publishers A Wholly Owned Subsidary of Trinity Broadcasting Network 2442 Michelle Drive Tustin, CA 92780

For information about special discounts for bulk purchases, please contact Trilogy Christian Publishing.

Manufactured in the United States of America

10 9 8 7 6 5 4 3 2 1

Library of Congress Cataloging-in-Publication Data is available.

ISBN 978-1-64088-243-0 (Paperback)
ISBN 978-1-64088-244-7 (ebook)

For you created my inmost being; you knit me
together in my mother's womb. I praise you
because I am fearfully and wonderfully made; your
works are wonderful, I know that full well.
Psalm 139:13-14 NIV

I Thank God for Elijah, Carter, Samuel, Maebry, Benjamin, Heidi

Blessings from God!

I Thank God for blazing sunsets

For clouds and springtime rains

I Thank God for bees and honey

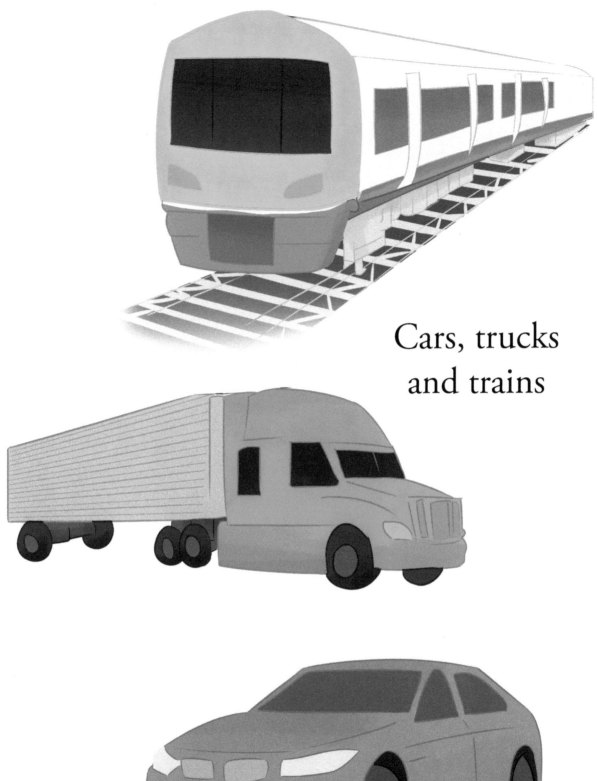

Cars, trucks
and trains

I Thank God for
snowcapped mountains

For oceans deep and blue

I Thank God for birds and flowers

Snakes and Lizards too

I Thank God for all His promises
For faith, hope and joy

I Thank God for every special
girl and boy

For each hair on your head
To the color of your eyes

For every different shape
And every different size

For each one was created
By our Father up above

And in you grows the seed
Of His love

CPSIA information can be obtained
at www.ICGtesting.com
Printed in the USA
BVHW020025130720
583533BV00001B/27

9 781640 882430